HAL•LEONARD DRUM PLAY-ALONG

weezer

VOL. 21

Cover photo by Karl Koch

Tracking, mixing, and mastering by
Jake Johnson & Bill Maynard at Paradyme Productions
Drums by Scott Schroedl
Guitars by Doug Boduch
Bass by Tom McGirr
Keyboards by Warren Wiegratz

T0101504

ISBN 978-1-4234-6316-0

HAL•LEONARD® CORPORATION

7777 W. BLUEMOUND RD. P.O. BOX 13819 MILWAUKEE, WI 53213

In Australia Contact:
Hal Leonard Australia Pty. Ltd.
4 Lentara Court
Cheltenham, Victoria, 3192 Australia
Email: ausadmin@halleonard.com.au

Visit Hal Leonard Online at
www.halleonard.com

VOL. 21

CONTENTS

Beverly Hills

Words and Music by Rivers Cuomo

Intro
Moderately slow Rock ♩ = 90

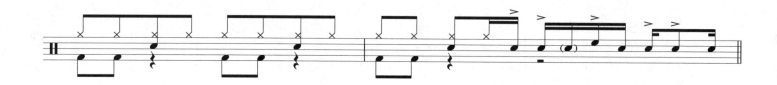

Verse

1. Where I ___ come from ___ is-n't all that great. My au-to-mo-bile ___ is a piece of

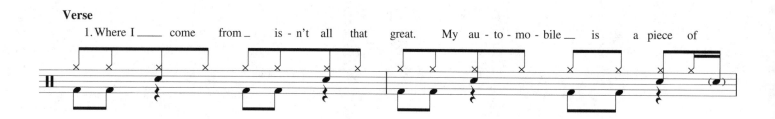

crap. My fash-ion sense ___ is a lit-tle whack ___ and my friends are just ___ as screw-y as

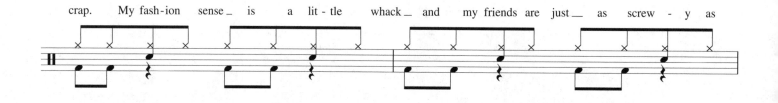

me. I did-n't go ___ to board - ing schools, ___ prep-py girls ___ nev-er looked at

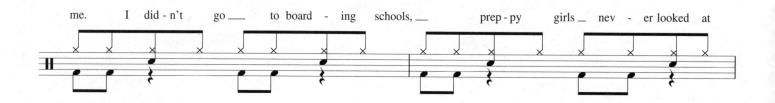

me. Why should they? I ain't no - bod-y, got noth-in' in my pock - et.

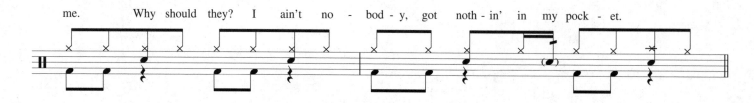

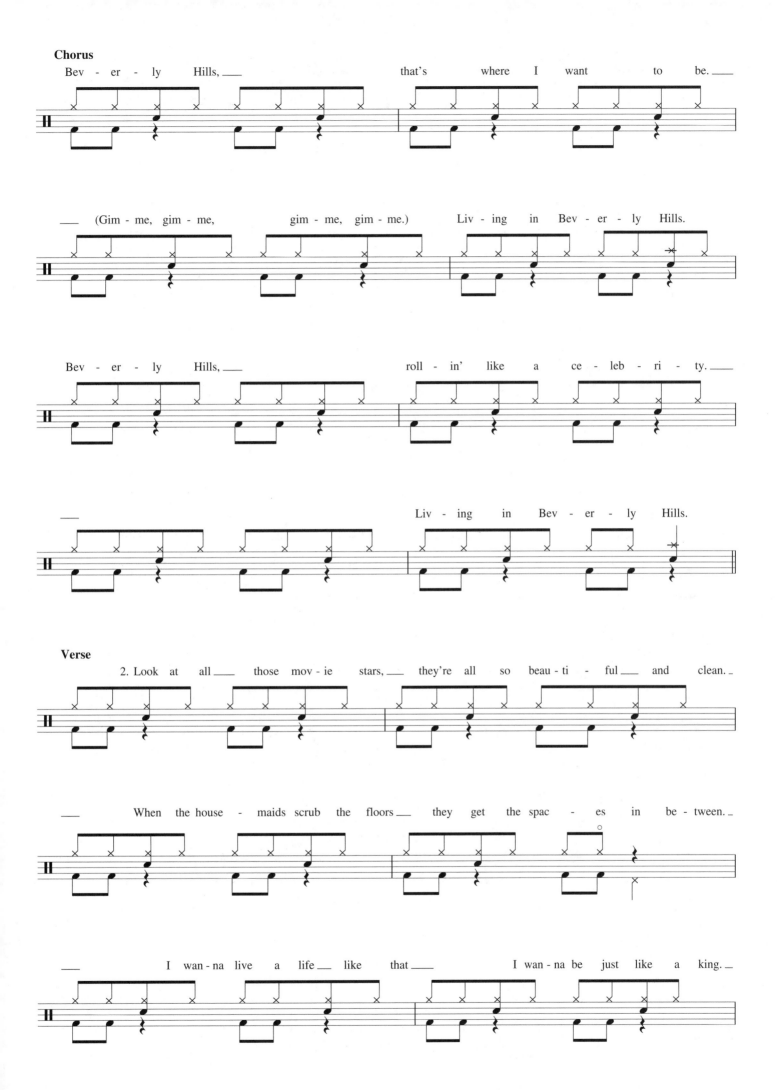

Take my pic - ture by ___ the pool ___ 'cause I'm the next big thing in...

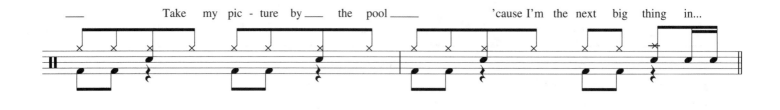

Chorus

Bev - er - ly Hills, ___ that's where I want to be. ___

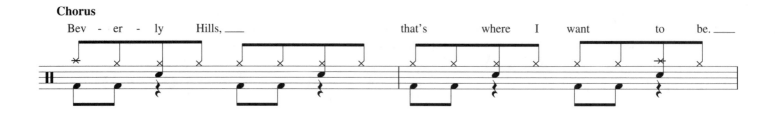

___ (Gim - me, gim - me, gim - me, gim - me.) Liv - ing in Bev - er - ly Hills.

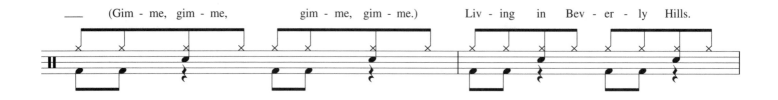

Bev - er - ly Hills, ___ roll - in' like a ce - leb - ri - ty. ___

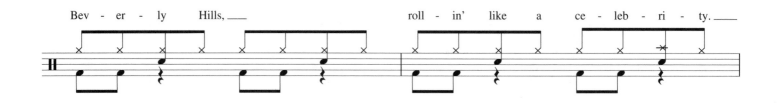

___ Liv - ing in Bev - er - ly Hills.

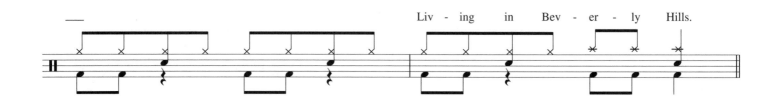

Guitar Solo

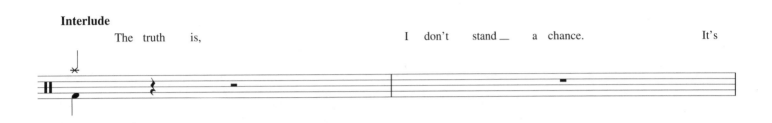

Interlude

The truth is, I don't stand __ a chance. It's

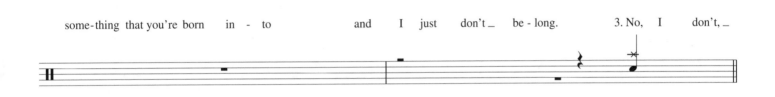

some-thing that you're born in - to and I just don't __ be - long. 3. No, I don't, __

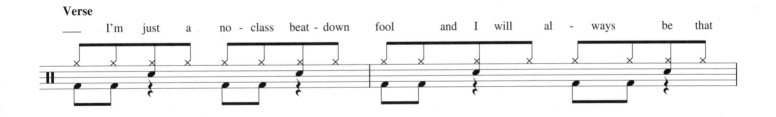

Verse

__ I'm just a no - class beat - down fool and I will al - ways be that

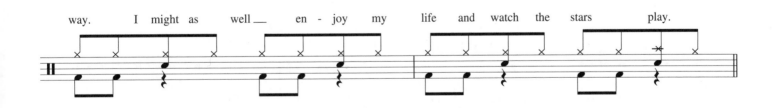

way. I might as well __ en - joy my life and watch the stars play.

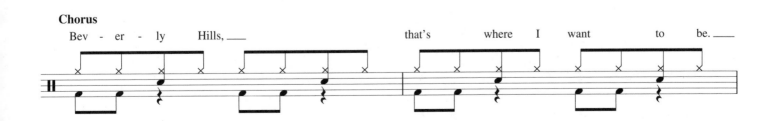

Chorus

Bev - er - ly Hills, ___ that's where I want to be. ___

(Gim - me, gim - me, gim - me, gim - me.) Liv - ing in Bev - er - ly Hills.

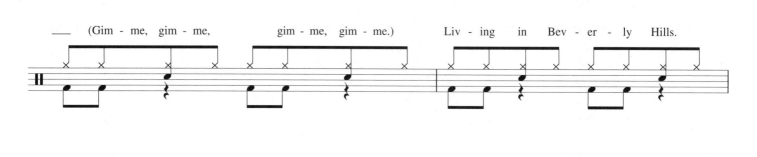

Bev - er - ly Hills, ____ roll - in' like a ce - leb - ri - ty. ____

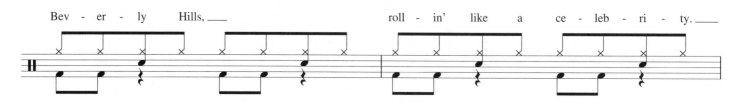

____ Liv - ing in Bev - er - ly Hills.

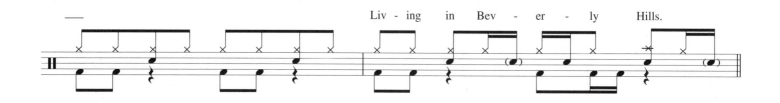

Outro-Chorus

Bev - er - ly Hills. ____

Bev - er - ly Hills. ____ Yeah!

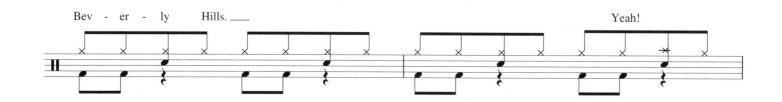

Bev - er - ly Hills. ____

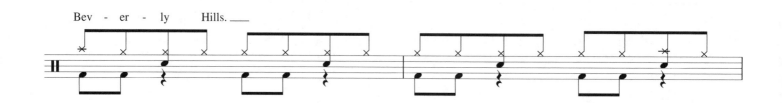

Bev - er - ly Hills. ____ Liv - ing in Bev - er - ly Hills.

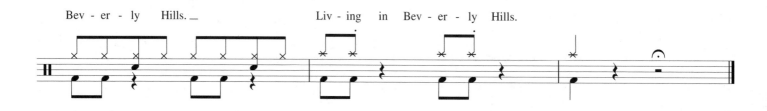

Hash Pipe

Words and Music by Rivers Cuomo

Intro
Moderate Rock ♩ = 128

1. I

𝄋 Verse

can't help my feel-ings, I'll go out of my mind. ___ These play-ers come to get me 'cause they'd
2. *See additional lyrics*

like my be-hind. ___ I can't love my busi-ness if I can't get a trick ___ down

on San-ta Mon-i-ca where tricks are for kids. ___ Oh, ___

Chorus

___ Come on and kick me. ___

Oh. ____

Come on and kick   me. ____

Come on and kick   me. ____

You got your prob - lems. ____

I got my eye   swipe. ____

You got your big   G's. ____   I got my hash   pipe. __

Interlude   *D.S. al Coda*

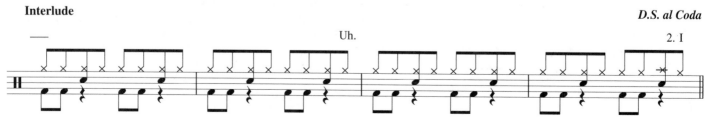

Uh.   2. I

Guitar Solo

*Open gradually, next 8 meas.

Oh. ___

Chorus

Come on and kick me. ___

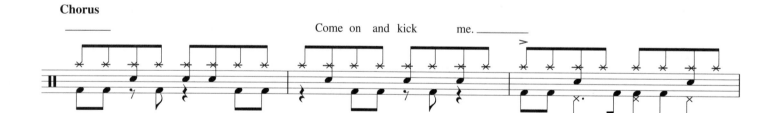

Oh. ___   Come on and kick me. ___

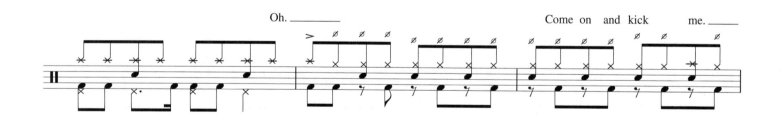

Come on and kick me. ___

Additional Lyrics

2. I can't help my boogies, they get out of control.
   I know that you don't care but I want you to know.
   The knee stocking flavor is a favorite treat
   Of men that don't bother with the taste of a teat.

Buddy Holly

Words and Music by Rivers Cuomo

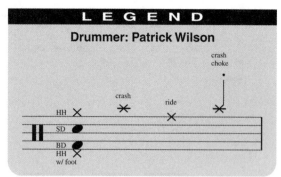

Mar - y Ty - ler Moore.   I   don't   care   what they   say   a - bout us   an - y - way. __

Interlude

I   don't   care 'bout   that.

Verse

2. Don't you ev - er __   fear,   I'm al - ways __   near.

I know that   you __   need   help. _____   Your tongue is   twist - ed,

your eyes are   slit. __   You need a   guard - i - an. _____

Pre-Chorus

(Woo - hoo.)   And you know __   I'm   yours. __   (Woo - hoo.)   And I   know __

____ you're mine. _   (Woo - hoo,   and that's __   for   all _____   time.) __

p ————————————————— *f*

Chorus

16

Guitar Solo

oh,   oh, — oh,   oh,   oh,   oh, oh. —

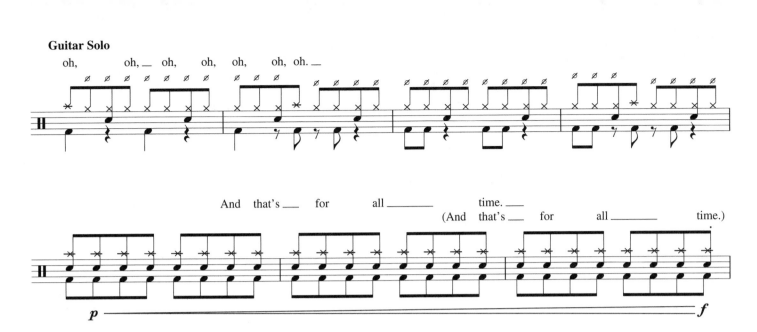

And that's — for   all ———— time. —
(And that's — for   all ———— time.)

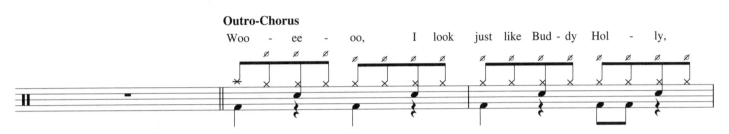

Outro-Chorus

Woo - ee - oo,   I look just like Bud - dy Hol - ly,

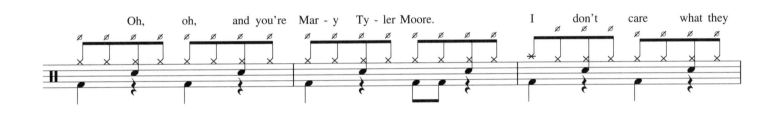

Oh,   oh,   and you're Mar - y Ty - ler Moore.   I   don't   care   what they

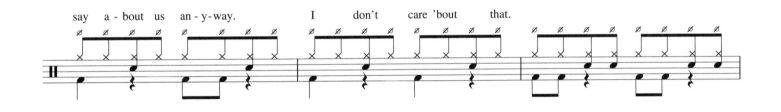

say a - bout us an - y - way.   I   don't   care 'bout   that.

I   don't   care 'bout   that.   I   don't   care 'bout   that.

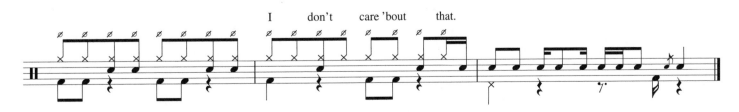

I   don't   care 'bout   that.

Dope Nose

Words and Music by Rivers Cuomo

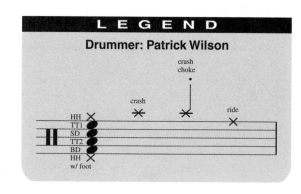

Intro
Moderate Rock ♩ = 132

(Guitar)

Ho, _____ oh, _____

_____ whoa, _____ oh. _____

Verse

1. Debt on ___ my head, wast - ing time on ___ my

own. Sleep, res - cue me, take ___ me

back to ___ my home.

Chorus

For the times that you wan - na go and ___ bust rhymes ___ real slow, _

Interlude

Verse

Chorus

For the times that you wan-na go and ___ bust rhymes ___ real slow, ___

I'll ap - pear, slap you on the face and ___ en - joy ___ the show. ___

___ This dope ___ nose.

Outro

Whoa, _____ oh, _____ oh. _____

Oo, oo, oo, oo, oo.

My Name Is Jonas

Words and Music by Rivers Cuomo, Jason Cropper and Patrick Wilson

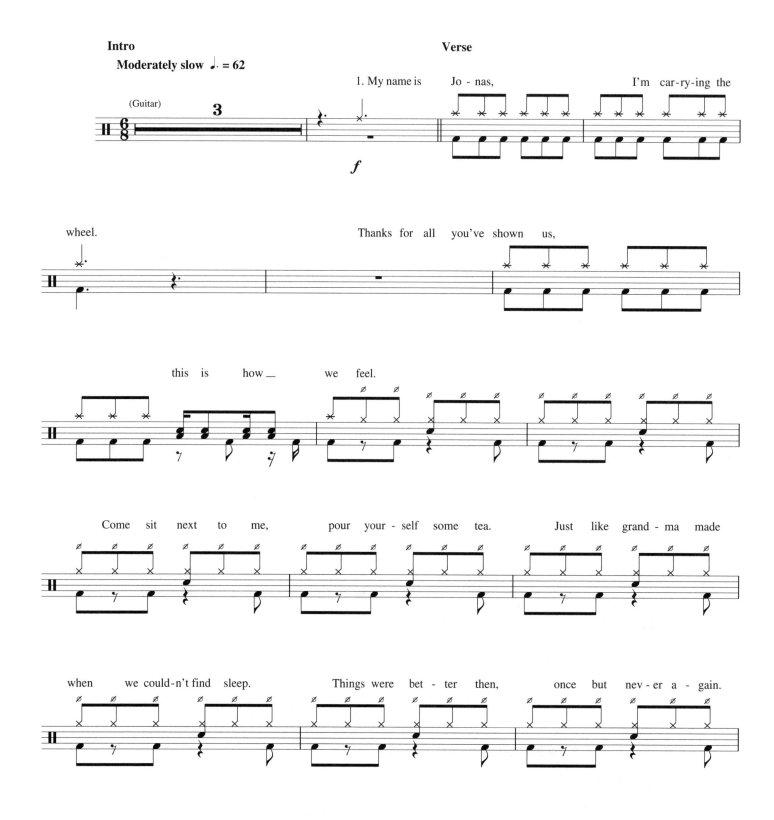

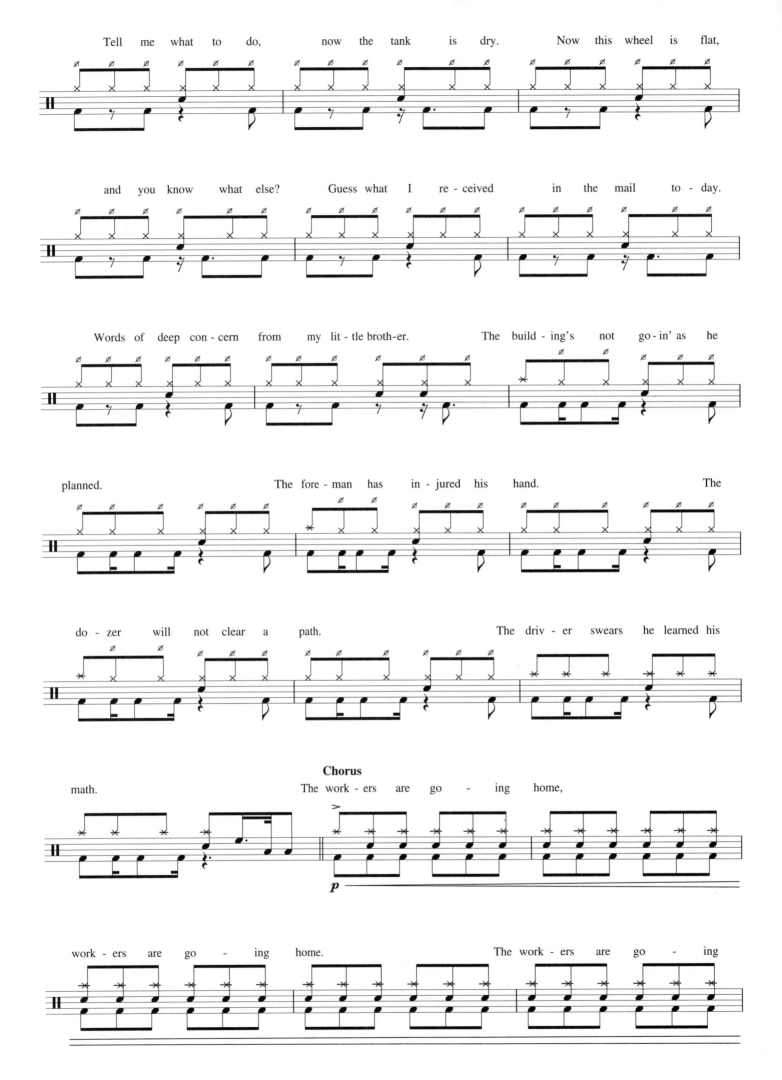

home, the work - ers are go - ing home.

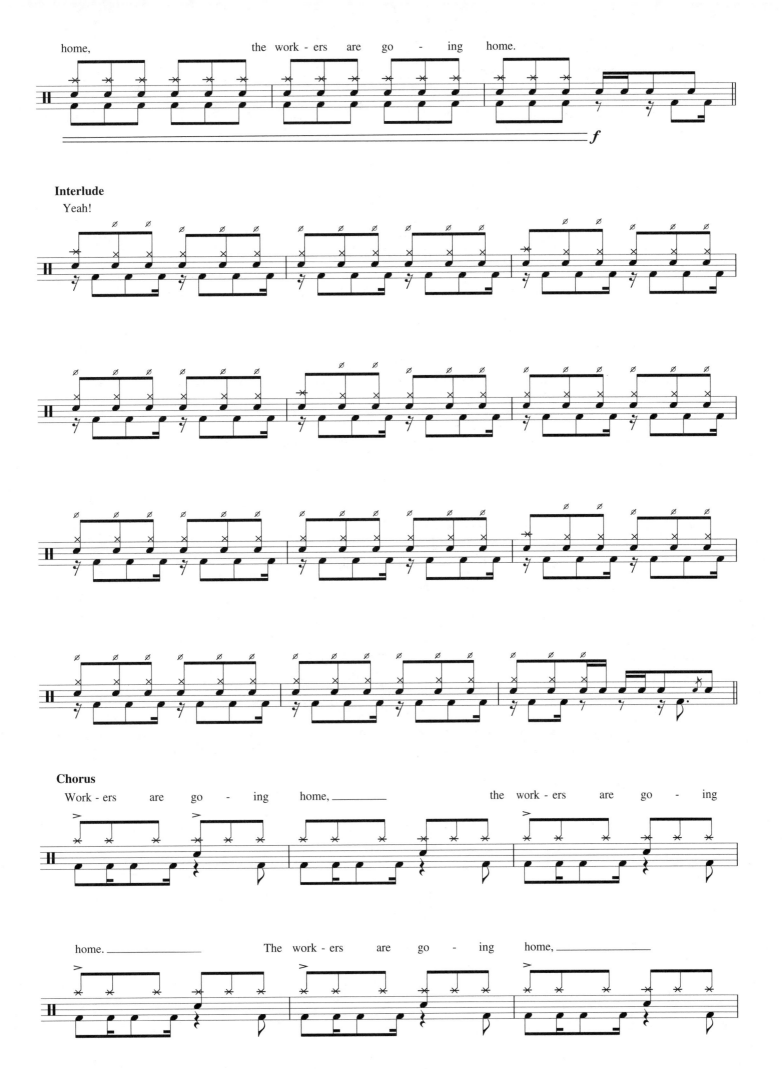

Interlude

Yeah!

Chorus

Work - ers are go - ing home, _____ the work - ers are go - ing

home. _____ The work - ers are go - ing home, _____

yeah,   yeah,   yeah.

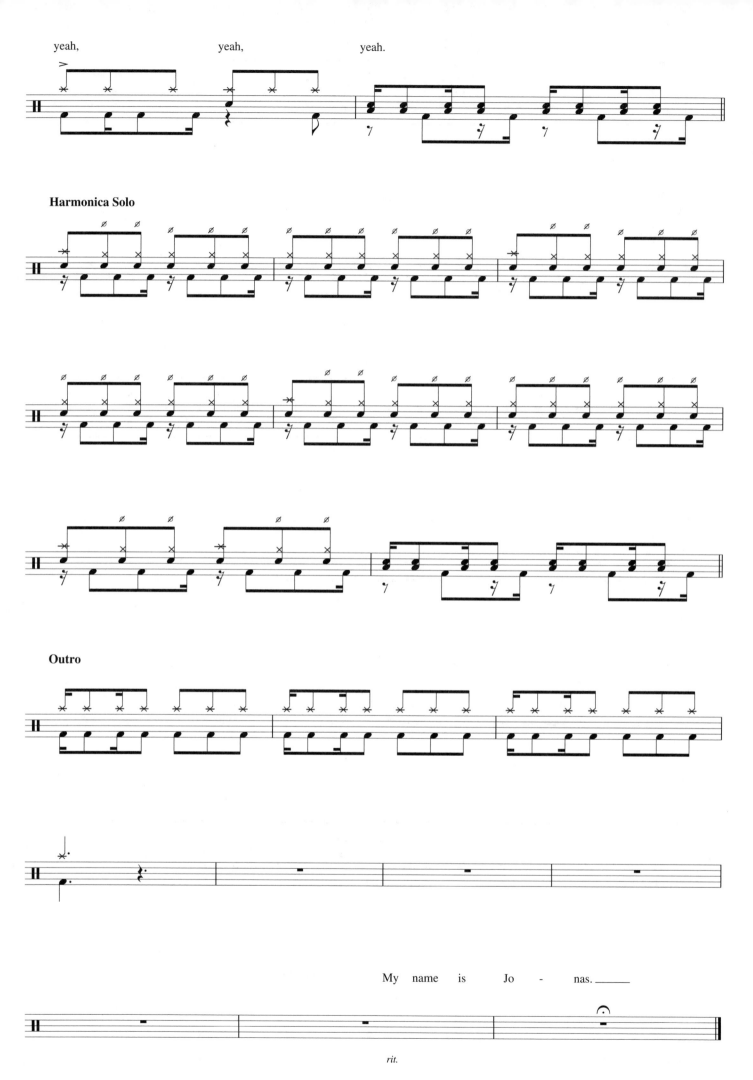

Harmonica Solo

Outro

My   name   is   Jo - nas. _____

rit.

Undone -
The Sweater Song

Words and Music by Rivers Cuomo

soon be nak - ed,   Ly - in' on the floor, _ I've come   un - done. _

Guitar Solo

Chorus

If   you   want   to de - stroy   my sweat-er, _   hold this   thread _ as   I

walk   a - way. _   Watch me un - rav - el,   I'll   soon   be   nak - ed.

Ly - in' on the floor, _   I've come   un - done. _   If   you want   to de -

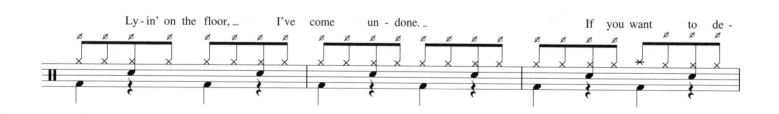

stroy   my sweat-er, _   hold this   thread _ as   I   walk   a - way. _

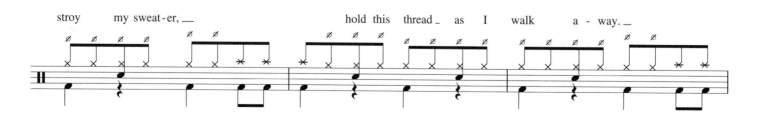

Watch me un-rav-el, I'll soon be nak-ed. Ly-in' on the floor, I've come un-done. _____

Outro

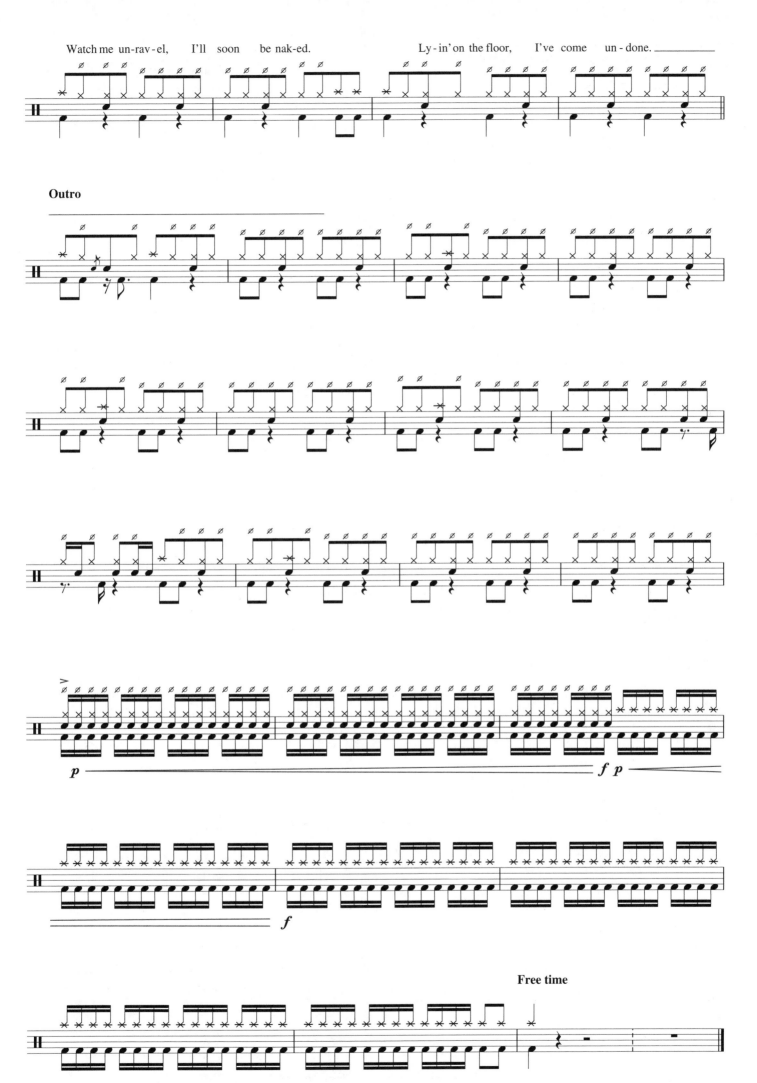

Free time

Pork and Beans

Words and Music by Rivers Cuomo

Intro
Moderately ♩ = 124

Verse

1. They say I need some Ro - gaine to put in my hair.

Work it out at the gym to fit my un - der - wear.

Oak - ley makes the shades to trans - form a tool.

You'd hate for the kids to think

that you lost your cool. I'm-a

Chorus

do the things that I wan - na do, I ain't got a thing to

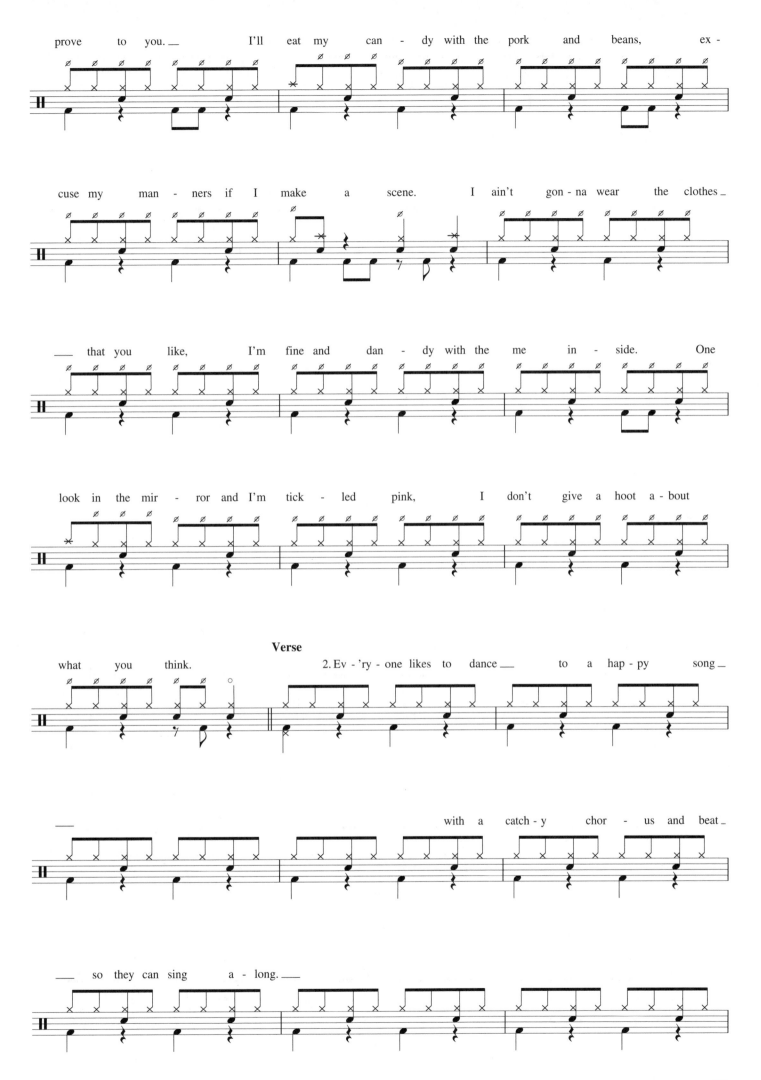

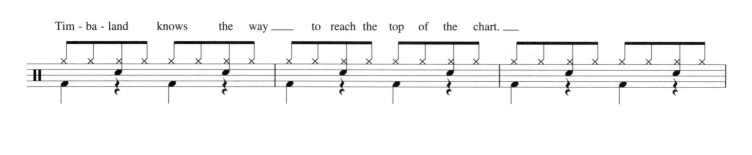

Tim - ba - land   knows   the   way ___ to reach the   top   of the   chart. ___

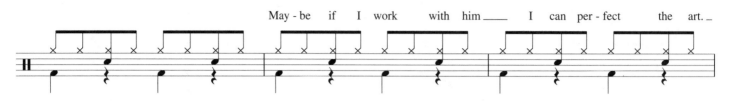

May - be   if   I   work   with   him ___ I   can per - fect   the   art. _

Chorus

I'm - a   do   the things _ that   I   wan - na   do, ___ I

ain't   got   a   thing   to   prove   to   you. ___ I'll   eat   my   can - dy   with the

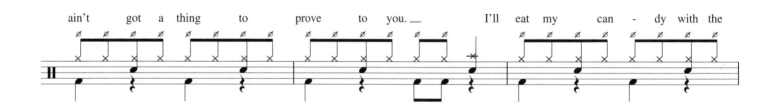

pork   and   beans,   ex - cuse   my   man - ners   if   I   make   a   scene.   I

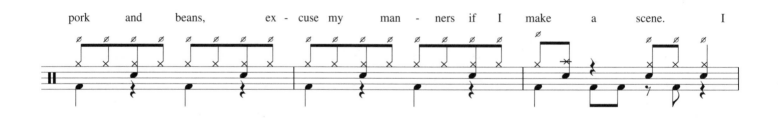

ain't   gon - na   wear   the   clothes ___ that   you   like,   I'm   fine   and   dan - dy   with the

me   in - side.   One   look   in   the   mir - ror   and   I'm   tick - led   pink,   I

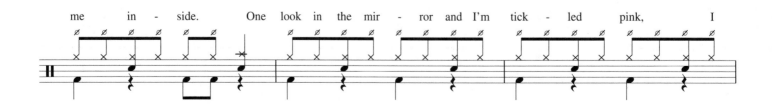

Bridge

Say It Ain't So

Words and Music by Rivers Cuomo

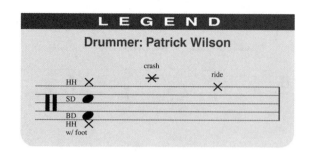

Intro
Slowly ♩ = 76

Oh,

 (Guitar)

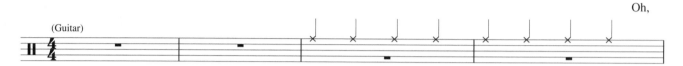

yeah. _ All right. _

Verse

1. Some-bod-y's heine - e is crowd-in' my ice - box.

Some-bod-y's cold __ one __ is giv-in' me chills. __

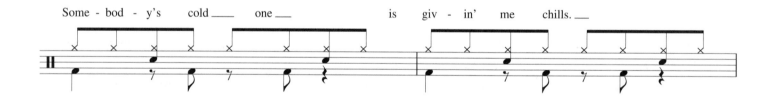

Interlude

Guess I'll just close _ my eyes. _ Oh, yeah. _ All

right. _ Feels good _ in - side. _

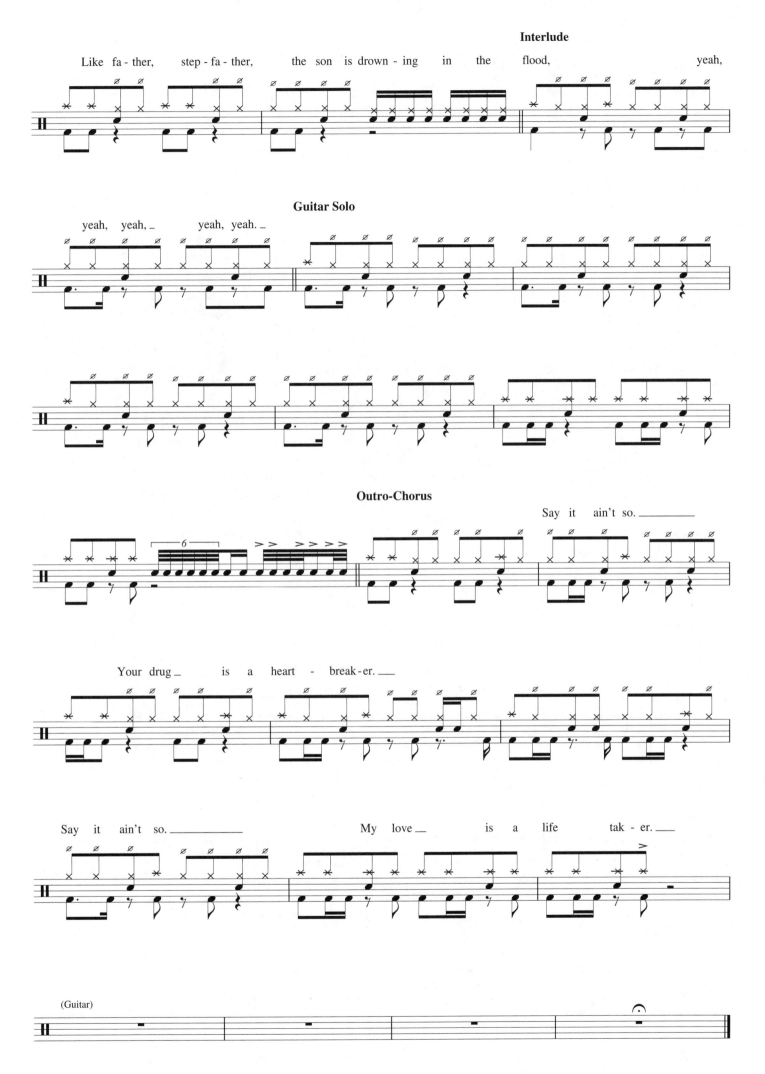

37